Date:

Time:

Weather:

Water Temperature:

Time in the water:

Companions:

Wows & After swim antics:

Date:

Time:

Weather:

Water Temperature:

Time in the water:

Companions:

Wows & After swim antics:

Date:

Time:

Weather:

Water Temperature:

Time in the water:

Companions:

Wows & After swim antics:

Date:

Time:

Weather:

Water Temperature:

Time in the water:

Companions:

Wows & After swim antics:

Date:

Time:

Weather:

Water Temperature:

Time in the water:

Companions:

Wows & After swim antics:

Date:

Time:

Weather:

Water Temperature:

Time in the water:

Companions:

Wows & After swim antics:

Date:

Time:

Weather:

Water Temperature:

Time in the water:

Companions:

Wows & After swim antics:

Date:

Time:

Weather:

Water Temperature:

Time in the water:

Companions:

Wows & After swim antics:

Date:

Time:

Weather:

Water Temperature:

Time in the water:

Companions:

Wows & After swim antics:

Date:

Time:

Weather:

Water Temperature:

Time in the water:

Companions:

Wows & After swim antics:

Date:

Time:

Weather:

Water Temperature:

Time in the water:

Companions:

Wows & After swim antics:

Date:

Time:

Weather:

Water Temperature:

Time in the water:

Companions:

Wows & After swim antics:

Date:

Time:

Weather:

Water Temperature:

Time in the water:

Companions:

Wows & After swim antics:

Date:

Time:

Weather:

Water Temperature:

Time in the water:

Companions:

Wows & After swim antics:

Date:

Time:

Weather:

Water Temperature:

Time in the water:

Companions:

Wows & After swim antics:

Date:

Time:

Weather:

Water Temperature:

Time in the water:

Companions:

Wows & After swim antics:

Date:

Time:

Weather:

Water Temperature:

Time in the water:

Companions:

Wows & After swim antics:

Date:

Time:

Weather:

Water Temperature:

Time in the water:

Companions:

Wows & After swim antics:

Date:

Time:

Weather:

Water Temperature:

Time in the water:

Companions:

Wows & After swim antics:

Date:

Time:

Weather:

Water Temperature:

Time in the water:

Companions:

Wows & After swim antics:

Date:

Time:

Weather:

Water Temperature:

Time in the water:

Companions:

Wows & After swim antics:

Date:

Time:

Weather:

Water Temperature:

Time in the water:

Companions:

Wows & After swim antics:

Date:

Time:

Weather:

Water Temperature:

Time in the water:

Companions:

Wows & After swim antics:

Date:

Time:

Weather:

Water Temperature:

Time in the water:

Companions:

Wows & After swim antics:

Date:

Time:

Weather:

Water Temperature:

Time in the water:

Companions:

Wows & After swim antics:

Date:

Time:

Weather:

Water Temperature:

Time in the water:

Companions:

Wows & After swim antics:

Date:

Time:

Weather:

Water Temperature:

Time in the water:

Companions:

Wows & After swim antics:

Date:

Time:

Weather:

Water Temperature:

Time in the water:

Companions:

Wows & After swim antics:

Date:

Time:

Weather:

Water Temperature:

Time in the water:

Companions:

Wows & After swim antics:

Date:

Time:

Weather:

Water Temperature:

Time in the water:

Companions:

Wows & After swim antics:

Date:

Time:

Weather:

Water Temperature:

Time in the water:

Companions:

Wows & After swim antics:

Date:

Time:

Weather:

Water Temperature:

Time in the water:

Companions:

Wows & After swim antics:

Date:

Time:

Weather:

Water Temperature:

Time in the water:

Companions:

Wows & After swim antics:

Date:

Time:

Weather:

Water Temperature:

Time in the water:

Companions:

Wows & After swim antics:

Date:

Time:

Weather:

Water Temperature:

Time in the water:

Companions:

Wows & After swim antics:

Date:

Time:

Weather:

Water Temperature:

Time in the water:

Companions:

Wows & After swim antics:

Date:

Time:

Weather:

Water Temperature:

Time in the water:

Companions:

Wows & After swim antics:

Date:

Time:

Weather:

Water Temperature:

Time in the water:

Companions:

Wows & After swim antics:

Date:

Time:

Weather:

Water Temperature:

Time in the water:

Companions:

Wows & After swim antics:

Date:

Time:

Weather:

Water Temperature:

Time in the water:

Companions:

Wows & After swim antics:

Date:

Time:

Weather:

Water Temperature:

Time in the water:

Companions:

Wows & After swim antics:

Date:

Time:

Weather:

Water Temperature:

Time in the water:

Companions:

Wows & After swim antics:

Date:

Time:

Weather:

Water Temperature:

Time in the water:

Companions:

Wows & After swim antics:

Date:

Time:

Weather:

Water Temperature:

Time in the water:

Companions:

Wows & After swim antics:

Date:

Time:

Weather:

Water Temperature:

Time in the water:

Companions:

Wows & After swim antics:

Date:

Time:

Weather:

Water Temperature:

Time in the water:

Companions:

Wows & After swim antics:

Date:

Time:

Weather:

Water Temperature:

Time in the water:

Companions:

Wows & After swim antics:

Date:

Time:

Weather:

Water Temperature:

Time in the water:

Companions:

Wows & After swim antics:

Date:

Time:

Weather:

Water Temperature:

Time in the water:

Companions:

Wows & After swim antics:

Date:

Time:

Weather:

Water Temperature:

Time in the water:

Companions:

Wows & After swim antics:

Date:

Time:

Weather:

Water Temperature:

Time in the water:

Companions:

Wows & After swim antics:

Date:

Time:

Weather:

Water Temperature:

Time in the water:

Companions:

Wows & After swim antics:

Date:

Time:

Weather:

Water Temperature:

Time in the water:

Companions:

Wows & After swim antics:

Date:

Time:

Weather:

Water Temperature:

Time in the water:

Companions:

Wows & After swim antics:

Date:

Time:

Weather:

Water Temperature:

Time in the water:

Companions:

Wows & After swim antics:

Date:

Time:

Weather:

Water Temperature:

Time in the water:

Companions:

Wows & After swim antics:

Date:

Time:

Weather:

Water Temperature:

Time in the water:

Companions:

Wows & After swim antics:

Date:

Time:

Weather:

Water Temperature:

Time in the water:

Companions:

Wows & After swim antics:

Date:

Time:

Weather:

Water Temperature:

Time in the water:

Companions:

Wows & After swim antics:

Date:

Time:

Weather:

Water Temperature:

Time in the water:

Companions:

Wows & After swim antics:

Date:

Time:

Weather:

Water Temperature:

Time in the water:

Companions:

Wows & After swim antics:

Date:

Time:

Weather:

Water Temperature:

Time in the water:

Companions:

Wows & After swim antics:

Date:

Time:

Weather:

Water Temperature:

Time in the water:

Companions:

Wows & After swim antics:

Date:

Time:

Weather:

Water Temperature:

Time in the water:

Companions:

Wows & After swim antics:

Date:

Time:

Weather:

Water Temperature:

Time in the water:

Companions:

Wows & After swim antics:

Date:

Time:

Weather:

Water Temperature:

Time in the water:

Companions:

Wows & After swim antics:

Date:

Time:

Weather:

Water Temperature:

Time in the water:

Companions:

Wows & After swim antics:

Date:

Time:

Weather:

Water Temperature:

Time in the water:

Companions:

Wows & After swim antics:

Date:

Time:

Weather:

Water Temperature:

Time in the water:

Companions:

Wows & After swim antics:

Date:

Time:

Weather:

Water Temperature:

Time in the water:

Companions:

Wows & After swim antics:

Date:

Time:

Weather:

Water Temperature:

Time in the water:

Companions:

Wows & After swim antics:

Date:

Time:

Weather:

Water Temperature:

Time in the water:

Companions:

Wows & After swim antics:

Date:

Time:

Weather:

Water Temperature:

Time in the water:

Companions:

Wows & After swim antics:

Date:

Time:

Weather:

Water Temperature:

Time in the water:

Companions:

Wows & After swim antics:

Date:

Time:

Weather:

Water Temperature:

Time in the water:

Companions:

Wows & After swim antics:

Date:

Time:

Weather:

Water Temperature:

Time in the water:

Companions:

Wows & After swim antics:

Date:

Time:

Weather:

Water Temperature:

Time in the water:

Companions:

Wows & After swim antics:

Date:

Time:

Weather:

Water Temperature:

Time in the water:

Companions:

Wows & After swim antics:

Date:

Time:

Weather:

Water Temperature:

Time in the water:

Companions:

Wows & After swim antics:

Date:

Time:

Weather:

Water Temperature:

Time in the water:

Companions:

Wows & After swim antics:

Date:

Time:

Weather:

Water Temperature:

Time in the water:

Companions:

Wows & After swim antics:

Date:

Time:

Weather:

Water Temperature:

Time in the water:

Companions:

Wows & After swim antics:

Date:

Time:

Weather:

Water Temperature:

Time in the water:

Companions:

Wows & After swim antics:

Date:

Time:

Weather:

Water Temperature:

Time in the water:

Companions:

Wows & After swim antics:

Date:

Time:

Weather:

Water Temperature:

Time in the water:

Companions:

Wows & After swim antics:

Date:

Time:

Weather:

Water Temperature:

Time in the water:

Companions:

Wows & After swim antics:

Date:

Time:

Weather:

Water Temperature:

Time in the water:

Companions:

Wows & After swim antics:

Date:

Time:

Weather:

Water Temperature:

Time in the water:

Companions:

Wows & After swim antics:

Date:

Time:

Weather:

Water Temperature:

Time in the water:

Companions:

Wows & After swim antics:

Date:

Time:

Weather:

Water Temperature:

Time in the water:

Companions:

Wows & After swim antics:

Date:

Time:

Weather:

Water Temperature:

Time in the water:

Companions:

Wows & After swim antics:

Date:

Time:

Weather:

Water Temperature:

Time in the water:

Companions:

Wows & After swim antics:

Date:

Time:

Weather:

Water Temperature:

Time in the water:

Companions:

Wows & After swim antics:

Date:

Time:

Weather:

Water Temperature:

Time in the water:

Companions:

Wows & After swim antics:

Date:

Time:

Weather:

Water Temperature:

Time in the water:

Companions:

Wows & After swim antics:

Date:

Time:

Weather:

Water Temperature:

Time in the water:

Companions:

Wows & After swim antics:

Date:

Time:

Weather:

Water Temperature:

Time in the water:

Companions:

Wows & After swim antics:

Date:

Time:

Weather:

Water Temperature:

Time in the water:

Companions:

Wows & After swim antics:

Date:

Time:

Weather:

Water Temperature:

Time in the water:

Companions:

Wows & After swim antics:

Date:

Time:

Weather:

Water Temperature:

Time in the water:

Companions:

Wows & After swim antics:

Date:

Time:

Weather:

Water Temperature:

Time in the water:

Companions:

Wows & After swim antics:

Date:

Time:

Weather:

Water Temperature:

Time in the water:

Companions:

Wows & After swim antics:

Date:

Time:

Weather:

Water Temperature:

Time in the water:

Companions:

Wows & After swim antics:

Date:

Time:

Weather:

Water Temperature:

Time in the water:

Companions:

Wows & After swim antics:

Date:

Time:

Weather:

Water Temperature:

Time in the water:

Companions:

Wows & After swim antics:

Date:

Time:

Weather:

Water Temperature:

Time in the water:

Companions:

Wows & After swim antics:

Date:

Time:

Weather:

Water Temperature:

Time in the water:

Companions:

Wows & After swim antics:

Date:

Time:

Weather:

Water Temperature:

Time in the water:

Companions:

Wows & After swim antics:

Date:

Time:

Weather:

Water Temperature:

Time in the water:

Companions:

Wows & After swim antics:

Date:

Time:

Weather:

Water Temperature:

Time in the water:

Companions:

Wows & After swim antics:

Date:

Time:

Weather:

Water Temperature:

Time in the water:

Companions:

Wows & After swim antics:

Date:

Time:

Weather:

Water Temperature:

Time in the water:

Companions:

Wows & After swim antics:

Date:

Time:

Weather:

Water Temperature:

Time in the water:

Companions:

Wows & After swim antics:

Date:

Time:

Weather:

Water Temperature:

Time in the water:

Companions:

Wows & After swim antics:

Date:

Time:

Weather:

Water Temperature:

Time in the water:

Companions:

Wows & After swim antics:

Date:

Time:

Weather:

Water Temperature:

Time in the water:

Companions:

Wows & After swim antics:

Date:

Time:

Weather:

Water Temperature:

Time in the water:

Companions:

Wows & After swim antics:

Date:

Time:

Weather:

Water Temperature:

Time in the water:

Companions:

Wows & After swim antics:

Date:

Time:

Weather:

Water Temperature:

Time in the water:

Companions:

Wows & After swim antics:

Date:

Time:

Weather:

Water Temperature:

Time in the water:

Companions:

Wows & After swim antics:

Date:

Time:

Weather:

Water Temperature:

Time in the water:

Companions:

Wows & After swim antics:

Date:

Time:

Weather:

Water Temperature:

Time in the water:

Companions:

Wows & After swim antics:

Date:

Time:

Weather:

Water Temperature:

Time in the water:

Companions:

Wows & After swim antics:

Date:

Time:

Weather:

Water Temperature:

Time in the water:

Companions:

Wows & After swim antics:

Date:

Time:

Weather:

Water Temperature:

Time in the water:

Companions:

Wows & After swim antics:

Date:

Time:

Weather:

Water Temperature:

Time in the water:

Companions:

Wows & After swim antics:

Date:

Time:

Weather:

Water Temperature:

Time in the water:

Companions:

Wows & After swim antics:

Date:

Time:

Weather:

Water Temperature:

Time in the water:

Companions:

Wows & After swim antics:

Date:

Time:

Weather:

Water Temperature:

Time in the water:

Companions:

Wows & After swim antics:

Date:

Time:

Weather:

Water Temperature:

Time in the water:

Companions:

Wows & After swim antics:

Date:

Time:

Weather:

Water Temperature:

Time in the water:

Companions:

Wows & After swim antics:

Date:

Time:

Weather:

Water Temperature:

Time in the water:

Companions:

Wows & After swim antics:

Date:

Time:

Weather:

Water Temperature:

Time in the water:

Companions:

Wows & After swim antics:

Date:

Time:

Weather:

Water Temperature:

Time in the water:

Companions:

Wows & After swim antics:

Date:

Time:

Weather:

Water Temperature:

Time in the water:

Companions:

Wows & After swim antics:

Date:

Time:

Weather:

Water Temperature:

Time in the water:

Companions:

Wows & After swim antics:

Date:

Time:

Weather:

Water Temperature:

Time in the water:

Companions:

Wows & After swim antics:

Date:

Time:

Weather:

Water Temperature:

Time in the water:

Companions:

Wows & After swim antics:

Date:

Time:

Weather:

Water Temperature:

Time in the water:

Companions:

Wows & After swim antics:

Date:

Time:

Weather:

Water Temperature:

Time in the water:

Companions:

Wows & After swim antics:

Date:

Time:

Weather:

Water Temperature:

Time in the water:

Companions:

Wows & After swim antics:

Date:

Time:

Weather:

Water Temperature:

Time in the water:

Companions:

Wows & After swim antics:

Date:

Time:

Weather:

Water Temperature:

Time in the water:

Companions:

Wows & After swim antics:

Date:

Time:

Weather:

Water Temperature:

Time in the water:

Companions:

Wows & After swim antics:

Date:

Time:

Weather:

Water Temperature:

Time in the water:

Companions:

Wows & After swim antics:

Date:

Time:

Weather:

Water Temperature:

Time in the water:

Companions:

Wows & After swim antics:

Date:

Time:

Weather:

Water Temperature:

Time in the water:

Companions:

Wows & After swim antics:

Date:

Time:

Weather:

Water Temperature:

Time in the water:

Companions:

Wows & After swim antics:

Date:

Time:

Weather:

Water Temperature:

Time in the water:

Companions:

Wows & After swim antics:

Date:

Time:

Weather:

Water Temperature:

Time in the water:

Companions:

Wows & After swim antics:

Date:

Time:

Weather:

Water Temperature:

Time in the water:

Companions:

Wows & After swim antics:

Date:

Time:

Weather:

Water Temperature:

Time in the water:

Companions:

Wows & After swim antics:

Date:

Time:

Weather:

Water Temperature:

Time in the water:

Companions:

Wows & After swim antics:

Date:

Time:

Weather:

Water Temperature:

Time in the water:

Companions:

Wows & After swim antics:

Date:

Time:

Weather:

Water Temperature:

Time in the water:

Companions:

Wows & After swim antics:

Date:

Time:

Weather:

Water Temperature:

Time in the water:

Companions:

Wows & After swim antics:

Date:

Time:

Weather:

Water Temperature:

Time in the water:

Companions:

Wows & After swim antics:

Date:

Time:

Weather:

Water Temperature:

Time in the water:

Companions:

Wows & After swim antics:

Date:

Time:

Weather:

Water Temperature:

Time in the water:

Companions:

Wows & After swim antics:

Date:

Time:

Weather:

Water Temperature:

Time in the water:

Companions:

Wows & After swim antics:

Date:

Time:

Weather:

Water Temperature:

Time in the water:

Companions:

Wows & After swim antics:

Date:

Time:

Weather:

Water Temperature:

Time in the water:

Companions:

Wows & After swim antics:

Date:

Time:

Weather:

Water Temperature:

Time in the water:

Companions:

Wows & After swim antics:

Date:

Time:

Weather:

Water Temperature:

Time in the water:

Companions:

Wows & After swim antics:

Date:

Time:

Weather:

Water Temperature:

Time in the water:

Companions:

Wows & After swim antics:

Date:

Time:

Weather:

Water Temperature:

Time in the water:

Companions:

Wows & After swim antics:

Date:

Time:

Weather:

Water Temperature:

Time in the water:

Companions:

Wows & After swim antics:

Date:

Time:

Weather:

Water Temperature:

Time in the water:

Companions:

Wows & After swim antics:

Date:

Time:

Weather:

Water Temperature:

Time in the water:

Companions:

Wows & After swim antics:

Date:

Time:

Weather:

Water Temperature:

Time in the water:

Companions:

Wows & After swim antics:

Date:

Time:

Weather:

Water Temperature:

Time in the water:

Companions:

Wows & After swim antics:

Date:

Time:

Weather:

Water Temperature:

Time in the water:

Companions:

Wows & After swim antics:

Date:

Time:

Weather:

Water Temperature:

Time in the water:

Companions:

Wows & After swim antics:

Date:

Time:

Weather:

Water Temperature:

Time in the water:

Companions:

Wows & After swim antics:

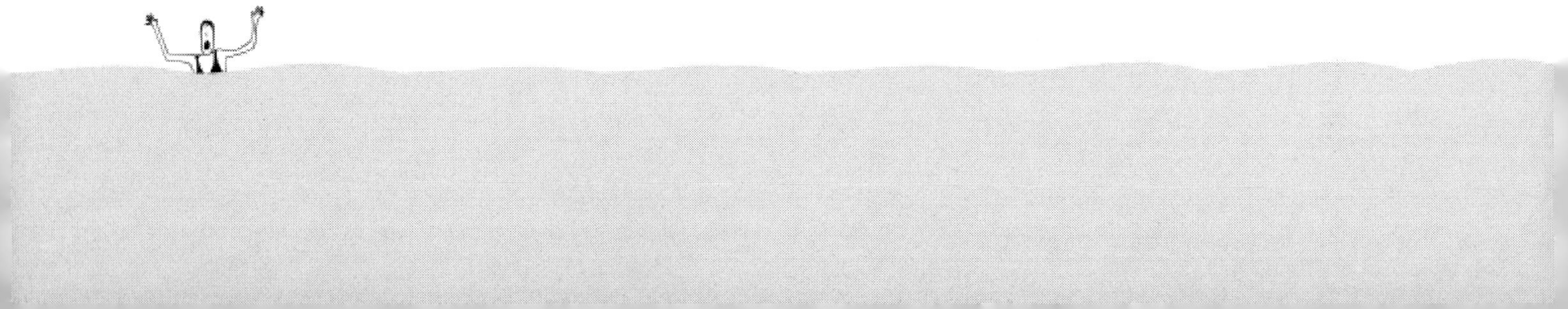

Printed in Great Britain
by Amazon

66008661R00121